COMMON CORE
LANGUAGE ARTS
GRADE 1

Suzanne Forbes

Lindsay Forbes

Common Core Education, Inc.
1695 Olinda Road
Makawao, Maui, HI 96768
www.CommonCoreEducation.com
ISBN-13: 978-0615514291
ISBN-10: 0615514294
©2011 Common Core Education, Inc.
Printed in the United States of America

Common Core State Standards for English Language Arts © Copyright 2010.
National Governors Association Center for Best Practices and Council of Chief
State School Officers. All rights reserved.

Graphics provided by Microsoft
Cover design by Jessica Matsumoto

TABLE OF CONTENTS

LANGUAGE STANDARD 1: Demonstrate command of the conventions of standard English grammar and usage when writing or speaking.

LANGUAGE STANDARD 2: Demonstrate command of the conventions of standard English capitalization, punctuation, and spelling when writing.

LANGUAGE STANDARD 4: Determine or clarify the meaning of unknown and multiple-meaning words and phrases based on *grade 1 reading and content*, choosing flexibly from an array of strategies.

LANGUAGE STANDARD 5: With guidance and support from adults, demonstrate an understanding of word relationships and nuances in word meanings.

Name _____

1. Tim is drinking a fizzy soda.

2. Mark does not like to clean his room.

3. Lucy and Simon share their toys with other children.

4. I like to read books with my father every Saturday.

5. Does Beth have an extra pencil?

6. I need a napkin to wipe my face.

7. Bill won a prize at the fair on Thursday.

8. How many pets does Lily own?

L.1.1.b   ©2011 Common Core Education, Inc.

Name _____

Circle all of the common nouns.

1. Ms. Kim has three pigs and one cow on her farm.

2. I can eat dessert after I finish my dinner.

3. My house and your house are on the same street.

4. Do you know how to ride a bike?

5. My family feeds the ducks at the park.

6. I like to hear rain falling on the roof.

7. My desk is next to Tia's desk.

8. Greg has brown hair and green eyes.

L.1.1.b

Name _____

1. My older sister Tina lives in New York City.

2. She likes to visit the Empire State Building.

3. Have you ever been to Times Square?

4. Some of the best plays are on Broadway.

5. There is great food in Little Italy and Chinatown.

6. I got a postcard from Tina on Thursday.

7. She was at the Bronx Zoo and saw lions.

8. You can go ice skating in Central Park when it is cold.

Name _____

1. My brother Ned is in first grade.

2. He goes to West Bend School on Main Street.

3. His favorite teacher is Mr. Chen.

4. On Thursday, Mr. Chen's class walked to the West Bend Park.

5. Mrs. Kimsey also went with her class.

6. The park is near the West Bend Library and the Super Saver Store.

7. Sheena and Dan ate lunch with Ned on the grass.

8. Ned and Dan said the trip to West Bend Park was a lot of fun.

L.1.1.b

Name _____

| Write the correct possessive noun on the blank. |

Example: The pencil belongs to Pam.

It is <u>Pam's</u> pencil.

1. The toy belongs to the baby.

It is the _____ toy.

2. The keys belong to my mother.

They are my _____ keys.

3. The dish belongs to the dog.

It is the _____ dish.

4. The pool belongs to Kamal.

It is _____ pool.

5. The books belong to Marco.

They are _____ books.

L.1.1.b

Name _____

Example: The fish belongs to Matt.

   It is <u>Matt's</u> fish.

1. The shoe belongs to Sanjay.

   It is _____ shoe.

2. The snack belongs to Tammy.

   It is _____ snack.

3. The horn belongs to that car.

   It is that _____ horn.

4. This dog belongs to Grandma.

   It is _____ dog.

5. These tools belong to Lauren.

   These are _____ tools.

Name _____

Rewrite each sentence. Remember to use a capital letter for each proper noun.

Example: Tomorrow jan will go to china.

Tomorrow Jan will go to China.

1. My aunt devina lives in texas.

_____

_____

2. Please give your homework to mr. woo.

_____

_____

3. I visit central zoo every year.

_____

_____

L.1.1.b   ©2011 Common Core Education, Inc.

Name _____

Example: The big top circus will visit our town.

The Big Top Circus will visit our town.

1. The name of the store is pet parade.

_____

_____

2. My uncle jose and aunt lori are here.

_____

_____

3. When will kurt go to canada?

_____

_____

Name _____

Example: The planet mars is far away.

<u>The planet Mars is far away.</u>

1. My dog damon chews on his bone.

_____

_____

2. Our principal is miss hassan.

_____

_____

3. They will visit japan and korea.

_____

_____

L.1.1.b
©2011 Common Core Education, Inc.

Name _____

Rewrite each sentence. Remember to use a capital letter for each proper noun.

Example: The name of the store is dollar days.

The name of the store is Dollar Days.

1. Do you live on cherry road?

_____

_____

2. We named our puppy scooby.

_____

_____

3. Does mick wear boots when it rains?

_____

_____

Name _____

1. The food store _____ down the street.

2. There _____ many foods on the shelf.

3. Apples and carrots _____ good for you.

4. The milk _____ next to the butter.

5. The bananas _____ next to the apples.

6. Where _____ the jelly?

7. The beans _____ not by the chips.

8. _____ the popcorn by the rice?

Name _____

1. My teacher (drive/drives) by my house.

2. The frogs (jump/jumps) into the pond.

3. The airplane (go/goes) into the clouds.

4. The children (eat/eats) their snacks.

5. The flowers (grow/grows) in the garden.

6. Sung and Andrew (walk/walks) to class.

7. We like to (talk/talks) to each other.

8. The cat (sit/sits) in the sun all day.

Name _____

1. Chaz (read/reads) in his room.

2. Pooja and Dan (play/plays) games together.

3. My brothers (share/shares) a room.

4. Alyssa does not (eat/eats) meat.

5. Zoe (go/goes) to soccer practice after school.

6. The monkey (jump/jumps) off the tree.

7. The rabbits (hop/hops) on the grass.

8. Did the bird (feed/feeds) its babies?

L.1.1.c

Name ___________________________

Write a verb (action word) on each blank to make this your own story. Try not to use a word more than once.

How to Get the Magic Lamp

First, you must _________________ into the forest. There will be monkeys that _________________, so be careful! You must _________________ on the stone path until you _________________ a cave. Next, _________________ into the cave. The lamp is inside! _________________ the lamp and _________________ away as fast as you can!

Name _____

1. I know that _____ always brushes his teeth.

2. Did _____ put away all of her toys?

3. Dan said _____ is a red car.

4. _____ is a nice girl.

5. Do you think _____ is a funny boy?

6. _____ is a silly cat.

7. You can put _____ on the table.

8. How many can _____ give to her brother?

L.1.1.d

Name _____

Write the word **I** or **we** to
complete each sentence.

1. _____ am very neat when I write.

2. Are _____ going to the classroom?

3. My dog knows when _____ am sad.

4. It is fun when _____ are at lunch.

5. _____ will always be friends.

6. When will _____ get to have my turn?

7. _____ like to work
together.

8. _____ am taller than
you.

L.1.1.d

Name _____

1. I like _____.

2. _____ are in the park together.

3. He said _____ are a good friend.

4. _____ need their jackets.

5. When are _____ going to ask your teacher?

6. _____ are funny clowns.

7. Their mothers will be upset if _____ get home late.

8. _____ are my best friend.

L.1.1.d

Name _____

1. _____ am the best swimmer.

2. _____ are the best runner.

3. When are _____ getting a new bike?

4. When it is cold _____ am not happy.

5. Tomorrow _____ am going to my grandfather's house.

6. If _____ are going to skate, then wear your helmet.

7. _____ am finished with my homework.

Name _____

1. The bike belongs to me. It is _____ bike.

2. The cat belongs to you. It is _____ cat.

3. The pencil belongs to you. It is _____ pencil.

4. The toy belongs to me. It is _____ toy.

5. The box belongs to you. It is _____ box.

6. The book belongs to you. It is _____ book.

L.1.1.d

Name _____

1. The snack belongs to the girl. It is _____ snack.

2. The pet belongs to him. It is _____ pet.

3. The pen belongs to Mrs. Watts. It is _____ pen.

4. The paper belongs to Uncle Charlie. It is _____ paper.

5. The scooter belongs to my sister. It is _____ scooter.

6. The boat belongs to my brother. It is _____ boat.

Name _____ .

1. The class belongs to us. This is
   _____ class.

2. Those books belong to them. Those
   are _____ books.

3. The house belongs to us. It is _____
   house.

4. That pool belongs to them. That is
   _____ pool.

5. The car belongs to them. That is
   _____ car.

6. These bananas belong to
   us. These are _____
   bananas.

Name _____

1. The toy car broke. _____ front wheel fell off.

2. The doctor told _____ mother I would be fine.

3. The monkey at the zoo sat inside _____ cage.

4. How long does a bear stay in _____ den?

5. I try _____ best all of the time.

6. Would you like to see _____ new baby sister?

7. The cat licked _____ fur.

Name _____

Write the word **I**, **me**, or **my** to complete each sentence.

1. _____ am in first grade.

2. Papa takes my sister and _____ to school every day.

3. _____ sister is in third grade.

4. After school, Nana asks me about _____ day.

5. Sometimes _____ tell her what I did in math.

6. Then Nana and _____ talk about homework.

7. She and Papa help my sister and _____.

    L.1.1.d

Name _____

Write the word **they** or **them** or **their** to complete each sentence.

1. Dana and Jamal ask me to play with _____ every day.

2. _____ are in my class.

3. I walk to school but _____ ride the bus.

4. When _____ bus gets to school, we walk to class together.

5. I do not mind waiting for _____.

6. _____ are my good friends.

7. My mother and _____ mothers are also friends.

8. So I get to see _____ a lot.

Name _____

1. Is there _____ in the car?

2. Thank you for _____!

3. I am full because I ate _____ on my plate.

4. School is fun for _____ who wants to learn.

5. _____ is on sale at the store.

6. Put _____ over there, please.

7. Do you think _____ will find the hidden treasure?

8. If _____ is put away, I can go outside to play.

            L.1.1.d

Name _____

1. When I am hungry I want to eat _____.

2. My mother needs to buy _____ from the store.

3. I am trying to find _____ to play with me.

4. _____ wants to borrow my crayons.

5. She wants _____ for dessert.

6. Do you know _____ who can snap?

7. _____ is better than nothing.

Name _____

1. I like to (walk/walked) to school.

2. Yesterday we (walk/walked) to school in the rain.

3. Tomorrow my sister (walk/will walk) home with her friend.

4. Last week I (play/played) basketball with my friend.

5. Next week I (play/will play) again.

6. Would you like to (play/will play) with us?

Name _____

Underline the correct word or phrase
in each sentence.

1. I do not (like/liked) big dogs.

2. When I was a baby, I (like/liked) to drink from a bottle.

3. I think my mother (like/will like) her present.

4. Did you (like/liked) the movie?

5. My uncle (like/will like) his new car.

6. Last year I (liked/will like) to swim in the pool.

7. How many scoops of ice cream would you (like/liked)?

L.1.1.e

Name _____

1. Homework is _____.

2. I am _____.

2. My bedroom is _____.

3. My shirt is _____.

4. The inside of my desk is _____ .

5. I like to eat _____ food.

6. _____ clothes are my favorite.

7. My _____ teacher helps us learn.

Name _____

Write an adjective (describing word) on each
blank to make this your own story.
Try not to use a word more than once.

My Toy Box

In my toy box, I have a _____
ball. It is _____ and _____.
I like to play with it when it is _____
outside. I also have a _____
toy car. It is _____. There are
also _____ blocks in my toy box.
I like to make _____ houses with
them. I also have crayons. I like to
make _____ and _____
pictures for my _____ friends.

Name _____

Example:

A **tiger** is <u>fast</u>, <u>striped</u>, <u>loud</u> and <u>orange</u>.

1. My **bed** is _____, _____, _____, and _____.

2. **Fireworks** are _____, _____, _____, and _____.

3. The **ocean** is _____, _____, _____, and _____.

Name _____

> Write adjectives (describing words)
> for each noun.

Example:

Turtles are <u>slow</u>, <u>green</u>, <u>shy</u>, and <u>quiet</u>.

1. A **party** is _____, _____, _____, and _____.

2. **Carrots** are _____, _____, _____, and _____.

3. A **fire truck** is _____, _____, _____, and _____.

Name _____

Circle the conjunction (connecting word) in each sentence.

Example: I munch on apples (and) bananas.

1. Katie and Darnell walk to school.

2. I want a book, but the library is closed.

3. I like to read because I learn new words.

4. We do not have milk, so we will got to the store.

5. Jake can wash the car or clean the dishes.

6. I need new shoes because my feet grew.

7. Do you want fish or pasta for dinner?

33   L.1.1.g   ©2011 Common Core Education, Inc.

Name _____

1. Red _____ blue are my favorite colors.

2. Choose one toy, the truck _____ the ball.

3. Is an apple _____ candy better for you?

4. Choose a snack, carrots _____ grapes.

5. I like both milk _____ juice.

6. Which one do you like better, this one _____ that one?

7. Did she go this way _____ that way when she left?

Name _____

1. I wanted to go to the store, _____ it was not open.

2. I am full _____ I ate a big lunch.

3. She left _____ it was time to go.

4. We can have pie, _____ we need to eat our dinner first.

5. I like green, _____ Ali likes blue.

6. My shoes are wet _____ I jumped in the puddle.

7. I can have a cat _____ not a dog.

8. We jumped in the lake _____ it was hot.

Name _____

Write **so** or **but** on the blank
to complete the sentence.

1. The store is open, _____ we will get bananas.

2. Meg reads _____ she can learn new words.

3. I do not like peas, _____ I know they are good for me.

4. There are extra snacks, _____ we can each have two.

5. My favorite color is red, _____ I also like green.

6. I will practice singing _____ I can get better.

L.1.1.g

Name _____

1. Do you have _____ pencil?

2. I have _____ itch.

3. Tuna is _____ type of fish.

4. How strong is _____ ox?

5. Martin wants to eat _____ orange.

6. I like to swim in _____ pool.

7. _____ animal can live in a zoo.

8. Take _____ umbrella in case it rains.

9. _____ mother is holding her baby.

L.1.1.g

Name _____

1. Have you ever been to _____ zoo?

2. _____ oven gets very hot.

3. Texas is _____ big state.

4. Is it smaller than _____ ant?

5. We will go see _____ movie today.

6. Tory wants to take _____ picture.

7. _____ apple is a good snack.

8. How many arms does _____ octopus have?

9. _____ rabbit hopped in the grass.

Name _____

Underline the correct word in each sentence.

1. Have you seen (this/these) picture?

2. (This/These) is a great day!

3. (This/These) snacks are yummy!

4. Jim, please put (this/these) book on the table.

5. Who will pick up all of (this/these) toys?

6. She said (this/these) is her favorite story.

7. I like (this/these) colors the best.

8. Which of (this/these) crayons do you want?

Name _____

Underline the correct word in each sentence.

1. Who fed (that/those) pig?

2. What is the name of (that/those) book?

3. I want to eat (that/those) bananas.

4. (That/Those) flags are from China and India.

5. We will visit (that/those) states.

6. (That/Those) are Ted's favorite toys.

7. (That/Those) grapes are very ripe.

8. Have you seen (that/those) movie?

9. (That/Those) fire is hot!

L.1.1.h

Name _____

Look at the picture. Then underline
the correct word in each sentence.

1. The bees fly (over/under) the
   flowers.

2. The cat is (over/under) the
   umbrella.

3. The frog sits (over/under) the
   clouds.

4. The girl jumps (over/under) the
   soccer ball.

L.1.1.i

Name _____

Look at the picture. Then underline the correct word or phrase in each sentence.

○□   1. The square is (over/next to) the circle.

□○   2. The square is (above/below) the circle.

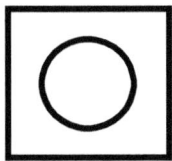

   3. The circle is (in/around) the square.

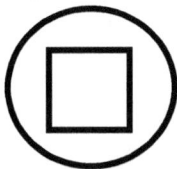

   4. The circle is (in/around) the square.

Name _____

Example: The car is fast.

The striped car is fast and colorful.

1. The dog sat.

_____

_____

2. Terry ran.

_____

_____

3. The duck swims.

_____

_____

4. School is fun.

_____

_____

L.1.1.j

Name ______________________________

Add words to expand the sentence.

Example: My bed is soft.

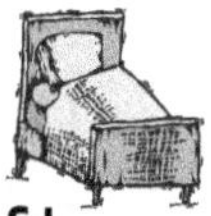

My cozy bed is soft and warm at night.

1. The frog jumped.

____

____

2. Brian walked.

____

____

3. I like toys.

____

____

4. Who ate my cookie?

____

____

Name _____

| Add words to expand the sentence. |

Example: Where is the party?

<u>Where is the super surprise party?</u>

1. My friend is nice.

_____

_____

2. When is the field trip?

_____

_____

3. The horse jumped.

_____

_____

4. What kind of ice cream do you want?

_____

_____

L.1.1.j

Name _____

Example: You ate my dessert!

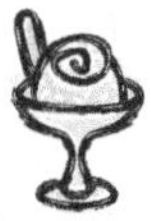

You ate my favorite dessert last night!

1. My sister is late!

_____

_____

2. Where is my teacher?

_____

_____

3. The clown ran.

_____

_____

4. Watch out for that monkey!

_____

_____

Name _____

> Circle the words in the sentence that should start with a capital letter.

1. my friend ed was born in april.

2. we do not have school on monday.

3. have you been to the west lake zoo?

4. mel watches sunday morning cartoons.

5. our dog's name is rover.

6. my brother brandon was born on january 10, 1993.

7. uncle bob and aunt sue live in tulsa.

8. does your sister mary live near fair view lake?

L.1.2.a

Name _____

Rewrite the date on the line.
Remember to use a capital letter.

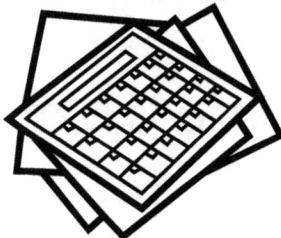

1. june 18, 1984

_____

2. october 24, 1965

_____

3. march 31, 2004

_____

4. july 7, 2011

_____

5. may 15, 2000

_____

Name _____

Write a **period (.)**, **question mark (?)**, or
exclamation point (!) at the end
of each sentence.

Example A: What time is lunch _?_

Example B: My soup is cold _._

1. I am ready to go to school ___

2. Can you count to 100 ___

3. I am so excited ___

4. My mother wears glasses ___

5. The chicken likes to eat corn ___

6. It is too hot today ___

7. What is your favorite game ___

8. Dad ate a hotdog at the party ___

9. That snake is really scary ___

L.1.2.b

Name _____

Write a **period (.)**, **question mark (?)**, or
exclamation point (!) at the end
of each sentence.

Example A: That really hurt **!**

Example B: The soccer ball is over there **.**

1. My father is a good cook ___

2. Did you take your cat to the vet ___

3. What is your name ___

4. I am so surprised ___

5. The library is closed for the day ___

6. When will they be back ___

7. How many kites are in the sky ___

8. Please take me with you ___

Name _____

1. july 4 2008

_____

2. november 20 1969

_____

3. may 5 1934

_____

4. february 9 1827

_____

5. march 1 2011

_____

6. july 16 1986

_____

L.1.2.c

Name _____

1. I like to play baseball soccer and kickball.

2. We paint draw and color in during art class.

3. Jang has three cousins named Sung Woo and Soo.

4. Apples bananas and berries and Derek's favorite fruits.

5. Today we had art math and reading.

6. Remember to stop look and listen before you cross the street.

Name _____

1. Red white and blue are the colors of the American flag.

2. Some flags have stripes stars or pictures.

3. Italy's flag is red white and green.

4. Yellow red and black are the colors on Germany's flag.

5. The flag of Chad has blue yellow and red stripes.

6. Some flags have stars moons or circles.

7. The color red is on the American Canadian and Chinese flags.

L.1.2.c

Name _____

1. Apples oranges and bananas are good to eat.

2. Lindsay was born on January 17 1990.

3. Eli has a truck a ball and a book in his toy box.

4. Do you want to wear a dress a skirt or shorts today?

5. Grandma was born on July 27 1936.

6. Toby plays with his brother sister and cousins.

7. Is your birthday in the spring summer or fall?

8. You can see the planets the moon and the stars in the sky.

Name _____

Underline the same root in each group of words.

Example: <u>add</u>s   <u>add</u>ed   <u>add</u>ing

1. steps   stepped   stepping
2. walks   walked   walking
3. looks   looked   looking
4. frowns   frowned   frowning
5. chirps   chirped   chirping
6. cooks   cooked   cooking
7. trips   tripped   tripping
8. yells   yelled   yelling
9. floats   floated   floating
10. stops   stopped   stopping
11. skips   skipped   skipping
12. plays   played   playing

L.1.4.c   ©2011 Common Core Education, Inc.

Name _____

Underline the same root in each group of words.

Example: <u>add</u>s   <u>add</u>ed   <u>add</u>ing

1. checks   checked   checking
2. jumps   jumped   jumping
3. flips   flipped   flipping
4. works   worked   working
5. washes   washed   washing
6. scrubs   scrubbed   scrubbing
7. watches   watched   watching
8. counts   counted   counting
9. follows   followed   following
10. turns   turned   turning
11. spells   spelled   spelling
12. point   pointed   pointing

Name _____

1. _____

2. _____

3. _____

4. _____

5. _____

Write a list of **clothes**.

1. _____

2. _____

3. _____

4. _____

5. _____

Name _____

Write a list of **fruits.**

1. _____

2. _____

3. _____

4. _____

5. _____

Write a list of **animals.**

1. _____

2. _____

3. _____

4. _____

5. _____

L.1.5.a

Name _____

Write a list of **sports.**

1. _____

2. _____

3. _____

4. _____

5. _____

Write a list of **snacks.**

1. _____

2. _____

3. _____

4. _____

5. _____

L.1.5.a

Name _____

Write the correct word from the word box on each blank to complete the sentence.

| vegetables | games | pets | desserts |

1. Carrots, potatoes, lettuce, and peas are all _____.

2. Pie, pudding, cake, and ice cream are all _____.

3. Cats, dogs, rabbits, and lizards are all _____.

4. Checkers, tag, cards, and kickball are all _____.

L.1.5.a

Name _____

wings	red	swims	stripes	round

1. A duck is a bird that _____.

2. A tiger is a large cat with _____.

3. A chicken has _____ and feathers.

4. A pie is a _____ dessert.

5. A fire truck is loud and _____.

Name _____

animals	pond	sour	soft	fly

1. A frog lives on land and near a

   _____.

2. A farm has plants and _____.

3. A lemon is _____ and yellow.

4. A cat is _____ and furry.

5. A bat has wings and can

   _____.

Name _____

Write a list of **foods that are sweet.**

1. _____

2. _____

3. _____

4. _____

5. _____

Write a list of **foods that are salty.**

1. _____

2. _____

3. _____

4. _____

5. _____

L.1.5.c

Name _____

Write a list of **places that are cozy.**

1. _____

2. _____

3. _____

4. _____

5. _____

Write a list of **animals that are furry.**

1. _____

2. _____

3. _____

4. _____

5. _____

L.1.5.c

Name _____

Circle the words that have almost the same
meaning as the word **look.**

peek	stop	glance	touch
stare	glare	feel	jump

Circle the words that have almost the same
meaning as the word **big.**

tiny	gigantic	huge	small
close	large	skinny	wide

65   L.1.5.d   ©2011 Common Core Education, Inc.

Name _____

Circle the words that have almost the same meaning as the word **jump.**

sit	leap	run	sleep
hop	rest	walk	bounce

Circle the words that have almost the same meaning as the word **dirty.**

dusty	clean	tidy	filthy
shiny	neat	messy	muddy

Page 1
1. soda
2. room
3. toys, children
4. books, father
5. pencil
6. napkin, face
7. prize, fair
8. pets

Page 2
1. pigs, cow, farm
2. dessert, dinner
3. house, house, street
4. you, bike
5. family, ducks, park
6. rain, roof
7. desk, desk
8. hair, eyes

Page 3
1. Tina, New York City
2. Empire State Building
3. Times Square
4. Broadway
5. Little Italy, Chinatown
6. Tina, Thursday
7. Bronx Zoo
8. Central Park

Page 4
1. Ned
2. West Bend School, Main Street
3. Mr. Chen
4. Thursday, Mr. Chen's, West Bend Park
5. Mrs. Kimsey
6. West Bend Library, Super Saver Store
7. Sheena, Dan, Ned
8. Ned, Dan, West Bend Park

Page 5
1. baby's
2. mother's
3. dog's
4. Kamal's
5. Marco's

Page 6
1. Sanjay's
2. Tammy's
3. car's
4. Grandma's
5. Lauren's

Page 7
1. My Aunt Devina lives in Texas.
2. Please give your homework to Mr. Woo.
3. I visit Central Zoo every year.

Page 8
1. The name of the store is Pet Parade.
2. My Uncle Jose and Aunt Lori are here.
3. When will Kurt go to Canada?

Page 9
1. My dog Damon chews on his bone.
2. Our principal is Miss Hassan.
3. They will visit Japan and Korea.

Page 10
1. Do you live on Cherry Road?
2. We named our puppy Scooby.
3. Does Mick wear boots when it rains?

Page 11
1. is
2. are
3. are
4. is
5. are
6. is
7. are
8. is

Page 12
1. drives
2. jump
3. goes
4. eat
5. grow
6. walk
7. talk
8. sits

Page 13
1. reads
2. play
3. share
4. eat
5. goes
6. jumps
7. hop
8. feed

Page 14
(Answers will vary.)

Page 15
1. he
2. she
3. it
4. She
5. he
6. It
7. it
8. she

Page 16
1. I
2. we
3. I
4. we
5. We
6. I
7. We
8. I

Page 17
1. you
2. They
3. you
4. They
5. you
6. They
7. they
8. You

Page 18
1. I
2. You
3. you
4. I
5. I
6. you
7. I

Page 19
1. my
2. your
3. your
4. my
5. your
6. your

Page 20
1. her
2. his
3. her
4. his
5. her
6. his

Page 21
1. our
2. their
3. our
4. their
5. their
6. our

Page 22
1. Its
2. my
3. its
4. its
5. my
6. m
7. its

Page 23
1. I
2. me
3. My
4. my
5. I
6. I
7. me

Page 24
1. them
2. they
3. they
4. their
5. them
6. They
7. their
8. them

Page 25
1. anyone
2. everything
3. everything
4. anyone
5. Everything
6. everything
7. anyone
8. everything

Page 26
1. something
2. something
3. someone
4. Someone
5. something
6. someone
7. Something

Page 27
1. walk
2. walked
3. will walk
4. played
5. will play
6. play

Page 28
1. like
2. liked
3. will like
4. like
5. will like
6. liked
7. like

Page 29
(Answers will vary.)

Page 30
(Answers will vary.)

Page 31
(Answers will vary.)

Page 32
(Answers will vary.)

Page 33
1. and
2. but
3. because
4. so
5. or
6. because
7. or

Page 34
1. and
2. or
3. or
4. or
5. and
6. or
7. or

Page 35
1. but
2. because
3. because
4. but
5. but
6. because
7. but
8. because

Page 36
1. so
2. so
3. but
4. so
5. but
6. so

Page 37
1. a
2. an
3. a
4. a
5. an
6. a
7. An
8. an
9. A

Page 38
1. a
2. An
3. a
4. an
5. a
6. a
7. An
8. an
9. A

Page 39
1. this
2. This
3. These
4. this these
5. this
6. these
7. these

Page 40
1. that
2. that
3. those
4. those
5. those
6. those
7. Those
8. that
9. That

Page 41
1. over
2. under
3. under
4. over

Page 42
1. next to
2. above
3. in
4. around

Page 43
(Answers will vary.)

Page 44
(Answers will vary.)

Page 45
(Answers will vary.)

Page 46
(Answers will vary.)

Page 47
1. My, Ed, April
2. We, Monday
3. Have, West Lake Zoo
4. Mel, Sunday
5. Our, Rover
6. My, Brandon, January
7. Uncle Bob, Aunt Sue, Tulsa
8. Does, Mary Fair View Lake

Page 48
1. June 18, 1984
2. October 24, 1965
3. March 31, 2004
4. July 7, 2011
5. May 15, 2000

Page 49
1. .
2. ?
3. !
4. .
5. .
6. !
7. ?
8. .
9. !

Page 50
1. .
2. ?
3. ?
4. !
5. .
6. ?
7. ?
8. .

Page 51
1. July 4, 2008
2. November 20, 1969
3. May 5, 1934
4. February 9, 1827
5. March 1, 2011
6. July 16, 1986

Page 52
1. I like to play baseball, soccer, and kickball.
2. We paint, draw, and color in art class.
3. Jang has three cousins named Sun, Woo, and Soo.
4. Apples, bananas, and berries are Derek's favorite fruits.
5. Today we had art, math, and reading.
6. Remember to stop, look, and listen before you cross the street.

Page 53
1. Red, white, and blue are the colors of the American flag.
2. Some flags have stripes, stars, or pictures.
3. Italy's flag is red, white, and green.
4. Yellow, red, and black are the colors on Germany's flag.
5. The flag of Chad has blue, yellow, and red stripes.
6. Some flags have stars, moons, or circles.
7. The color red is on the American, Canadian, and Chinese flags.

Page 54
1. Apples, oranges, and bananas are good to eat.
2. Lindsay was born on January 17, 1990.
3. Eli has a truck, a ball, and a book in his toy box.
4. Do you want to wear a dress, a skirt, or shorts today?
5. Grandma was born on July 27, 1936.
6. Toby plays with his brother, sister, and cousins.
7. Is your birthday in the spring, summer, or fall?
8. You can see the planets, the moon, and the stars in the sky.

Page 55
1. step
2. walk
3. look
4. frown
5. chirp
6. cook
7. trip
8. yell
9. float
10. stop
11. skip
12. play

Page 56
1. check
2. jump
3. flip
4. work
5. wash
6. scrub
7. watch
8. count
9. follow
10. turn
11. spell
12. point

Page 57
(Answers will vary.)

Page 58
(Answers will vary.)

Page 59
(Answers will vary.)

Page 60
1. vegetables
2. desserts
3. pets
4. games

Page 61
1. swims
2. stripes
3. wings
4. round
5. red

Page 62
1. pond
2. animals
3. sour
4. soft
5. fly

Page 63
(Answers will vary.)

Page 64
(Answers will vary.)

Page 65
look: peak, glance, stare, glare
big: gigantic, huge, large, wide

Page 66
jump: leap, hop, bounce
dirty: dusty, filthy, messy, muddy